Kim the Boss
and
Less and Less

Level 2 – Red

Helpful Hints for Reading at Home

The graphemes (written letters) and phonemes (units of sound) used throughout this series are aligned with Letters and Sounds. This offers a consistent approach to learning whether reading at home or in the classroom.

HERE IS A LIST OF PHONEMES FOR THIS PHASE OF LEARNING. AN EXAMPLE OF THE PRONUNCIATION CAN BE FOUND IN BRACKETS.

Phase 2			
s (sat)	a (cat)	t (tap)	p (tap)
i (pin)	n (net)	m (man)	d (dog)
g (go)	o (sock)	c (cat)	k (kin)
ck (sack)	e (elf)	u (up)	r (rabbit)
h (hut)	b (ball)	f (fish)	ff (off)
l (lip)	ll (ball)	ss (hiss)	

HERE ARE SOME WORDS WHICH YOUR CHILD MAY FIND TRICKY.

Phase 2 Tricky Words			
the	to	I	no
go	into		

TOP TIPS FOR HELPING YOUR CHILD TO READ:

- Allow children time to break down unfamiliar words into units of sound and then encourage children to string these sounds together to create the word.

- Encourage your child to point out any focus phonics when they are used.

- Read through the book more than once to grow confidence.

- Ask simple questions about the text to assess understanding.

- Encourage children to use illustrations as prompts.

London Borough of Enfield	
91200000774752	
Askews & Holts	07-Sep-2022
JF YGN BEGINNER READE	
ENSOUT	

PHASE 2 /ss/

This book focuses on the phoneme /ss/ and is a red level 2 book band.

Kim the Boss
and
Less and Less

Written by
William Anthony

Illustrated by
Danielle Webster-Jones

Can you say this sound and draw it with your finger?

Kim the Boss

Written by
William Anthony

Illustrated by
Danielle Webster-Jones

Kim is the boss.

It is no fuss as the boss.

The boss can go, "No!"

Tess is in.

"Kim, can I hiss?"

"No."
Kim is the boss.

"Kim, can I kick it?"

"No."
Kim is the boss.

But the boss has a boss.

Mum is in. Mum is mad.

"It is a mess, Kim."

It is a lot of fuss as the boss.

How many words can you think of that contain **ss**? Here are some to get you started…

Less and Less

Written by
William Anthony

Illustrated by
Danielle Webster-Jones

It is Ross. Ross sits.

"Go," huffs Ross.

Bob is off.

It is fab. It is no fuss.

"No. Less," huffs Ross.

"But less is a no go," sobs Bob.

"Less," huffs Ross.

Bob rubs and rubs. It is a mess.

"Less," huffs Ross.

Bob rubs and rubs. It is a big mess.

It is Ross.

But Bob is in a huff.

©2022 **BookLife Publishing Ltd.**
King's Lynn, Norfolk, PE30 4LS, UK

ISBN 978-1-80155-798-6

All rights reserved. Printed in Poland.
A catalogue record for this book is available from the British Library.

Kim the Boss and Less and Less
Written by William Anthony
Illustrated by Danielle Webster-Jones

An Introduction to BookLife Readers...

Our Readers have been specifically created in line with the London Institute of Education's approach to book banding and are phonetically decodable and ordered to support each phase of Letters and Sounds.

Each book has been created to provide the best possible reading and learning experience. Our aim is to share our love of books with children, providing both emerging readers and prolific page-turners with beautiful books that are guaranteed to provoke interest and learning, regardless of ability.

BOOK BAND GRADED using the Institute of Education's approach to levelling.

PHONETICALLY DECODABLE supporting each phase of Letters and Sounds.

EXERCISES AND QUESTIONS to offer reinforcement and to ascertain comprehension.

BEAUTIFULLY ILLUSTRATED to inspire and provoke engagement, providing a variety of styles for the reader to enjoy whilst reading through the series.

AUTHOR INSIGHT:
WILLIAM ANTHONY

William Anthony's involvement with children's education is quite extensive. He has written and edited many titles for BookLife Publishing across a wide range of subjects. William graduated from Cardiff University with a 1st Class BA (Hons) in Journalism, Media and Culture, creating an app and a TV series, among other things, during his time there.

William Anthony has also produced work for the Prince's Trust, a charity created by HRH The Prince of Wales, that helps young people with their professional future. He has created animated videos for a children's education company that works closely with the charity.

PHASE 2 /ss/

This book focuses on the phoneme /ss/ and is a red level 2 book band.